Soft Thunder

BRITISH HAIKU SOCIETY

FOUNDED 1990

Printers:
BookPrintingUK
Remus House, Coltsfoot Drive,Woodston
Peterborough PE2 9BF

Judges: Beverley George & Ron Woollard

Competition Administrators: Claire Knight
                                   & Andrew Shimield

Editor: Frank Williams

Published by:-

The British Haiku Society,
Flat 4,
2 Clifton Lawns,
Ramsgate,
Kent CT11 9PB

(www.britishhaikusociety.org.uk/anotherkind
ofpoetry/anotherkind/slideshow)

Additional copies of this anthology are available at the
cost of £4.00 (including p&p) from the Membership
Secretary.

Introduction - Year of Tanka

2014 was a Year of Tanka for the British Haiku Society and, as part of this endeavour to promote tanka writing, the first BHS Tanka Anthology Competition was held.

This well-supported contest drew 74 entrants from 15 countries*, providing us with 245 tanka. From these entries 47 have been selected by judges Beverley George (Aus) and Ron Woollard (UK) for the Anthology, after several weeks' careful and enthusiastic deliberation!

The following pages contain the successful entrants' previously unpublished poems. It can truly be said to be, a world-wide effort. We hope you find them of great interest, thought-provoking and, perhaps above all, enjoyable. Many thanks to all who participated in this competition.

*Breakdown of entrants:

UK 42	New Zealand 1
USA 8	Croatia 1
Germany 2	France 1
Australia 7	Switzerland 1
Hungary 1	India 1
Canada 4	Mexico 1
Slovenia 1	&
Ireland 2	Japan 1

Competition Administrators: Claire Knight
& Andrew Shimield

Foreword

There was an overwhelming response to this competition for inclusion in the BHS Tanka Anthology. A pleasing result because it shows the high degree of interest that exists for the genre. At the same time it caused something of a challenge for the judges.

In making their choices the judges felt that, while adopting a fairly liberal approach, there must be some differentiation between a short poem and a tanka. If there is none, then the genre ceases to exist as a separate entity and becomes a small part of the body of English poetry, in which a poem is written in five lines.

No one should expect an exact definition, any more than there is a consensus of what a haiku is, but both judges felt that there should be at least a respectful nod in the direction of the tanka's ancient origins. This includes a recognisable structure — not necessarily 5-7-5-7-7, which does not reflect the intrinsic linguistic differences between Japanese and English, but a structure that reflects this pattern of line length. One also in which there is some turning point or juxtaposition of images and viewpoint.

The tanka should also have a lyrical flow of words, best demonstrated when read aloud. At the same time it should make an emotional impact on the reader, often bringing new insights into human experience or uncovering unlooked for humour.

Having said this, the judges would like to thank those who submitted items not included in this anthology.

Some of these, after much discussion between the judges, were reluctantly omitted as not being tanka, but nevertheless were interesting short poems which gave the judges much pleasure in reading.

Judges: Beverley George and Ron Woollard

First Prize

> fathers' race
> arms and legs flailing
> hearts pumping
> even now, even here,
> it matters

> Catherine Redfern
> (UK)

Judges' Report:

Beverley George: From the first reading, this tanka was memorable and convincing. It says so much, so simply.

Ron Woollard: This was chosen by both judges independently for first place. It has an easy flow of words with a touch of humour, poking gentle fun at the human condition. Its simplicity gives it added strength.

Second Prize

> through the face
> of an aged war veteran
> the fighter pilot speaks
> —the sound of soft thunder
> quivers a thin moon

> Linda Jeannette Ward
> (USA)

Judges' Report:

Beverley George: The contrasting images of the night sky made fluid as thunder announces a storm and the traces of the younger man detected at times in the veteran's face are delicately counterpoised. The sound of gunfire is suggested, but subtly.

Ron Woollard: The last two lines create an arresting and haunting image to link with the first three.

Joint Third Prize

> harbour bridge
> the expanse of cold steel
> above and below
> so many years together
> so much space between us

> Vanessa Proctor
> (Australia)

Judges' Report:

Ron Woollard: The imagery of the first three lines linking with the last two is striking.

Beverley George: A well-structured tanka, balanced to suit the subject.

Joint Third Prize

stunned
by the lily's whiteness
i search
for another way
to say goodbye

Doreen King
(UK)

Judges' Report:

Ron Woollard: The tanka reflects the inadequate way we try to deal with bereavement **after the poet's** sudden reaction to seeing white lilies.

Beverley George: So often funeral formalities seem unrelated to the deceased person we have loved. Elegantly and sparely expressed, this tanka conveys a depth of emotion most readers will recognise.

Highly Commended

if only these echoes
led straight to you
haunting each space
the senseless search
of empty rooms

Joanna Ashwell
(UK)

Judges' Report:

Ron Woollard: Strong imagery in this that emphasizes the sense of loss.

Beverley George: Carefully chosen words to convey the sense of deep loss.

Highly Commended

abandoning
all that went before
I walk miles and miles of shore
watch a swell of scoters
catch and release the sky

Linda Jeannette Ward
(USA)

Judges' Report:

Ron Woollard: Strongly poetic tanka, is particularly fluent. The last line is a memorable image.

Beverley George: Nature as an emancipating, healing force. A pleasing poem to read aloud.

Commended

> my father's
> beloved *Ivanhoe*—
> flakes of tobacco
> fall from pages
> no longer turned
>
> Catherine Redfern
> (UK)

Judges' Report:

Ron Woollard: Simple yet moving it captures a moment full of meaning.

Beverley George: Time and place recaptured

Commended

wild geese landing
between the ploughed land's furrows
in his dream
the refugee still flying
with his daughter in the arms

Judit K. Hollos
(Hungary)

Judges' Report:

Ron Woollard: A moving tanka with powerful imagery.

Beverley George: Another poem I found emotionally convincing. The imagery of the first two lines juxtaposes well with the refugee's haunted dream while the third line serves as a pivot that can be read with either the first two or last two lines.

Commended

> an army
> of wind turbines
> marching out
> across the fields
> across my dreams
>
> John Soules
> (Canada)

Judges' Report:

Beverley George: The image of turbines, although providing green power, intruding on and forever changing a formerly loved landscape is simply stated. The powerlessness of the writer is indicated by the word 'army' and the repeated word 'across'.

Ron Woollard: A point of view strongly made, the last line is particularly effective.

Commended

> wingtip to wingtip
> the albatross pair
> perfects its dance...
> the burden of not knowing
> will you go first, or I ?
>
> Claire Everett
> (UK)

Judges' Report:

Ron Woollard: Well observed nature in action, the last two lines make for an interesting connection.

Beverley George: Imaginative word choice and imagery bring fresh interest to this not uncommon theme. The tanka is lyrical and rewards reading aloud.

Commended

> with rainsong
> whispering in my ear
> how could I
> not have known that
> the time had come for leaving
>
>> Debbie Strange
>> (Canada)

Judges' Report:

Ron Woollard: The sense of melancholy and sadness is delicately drawn.

Beverley George: The sorrow of parting delicately expressed.

Runners-up

I strain to read
the doctor's handwriting
on the clipboard
something about morphine
and no heroic measures

    Tracy Davidson
    (UK)

sleepless night
there aren't enough sheep
in the world
the empty space beside me
feels emptier

    Tracy Davidson
    (UK)

Runners-up

autumn sycamores
raining gold on wet asphalt
you are beautiful
he's told me so often
it's begun to stick

    Claire Everett
    (UK)

late afternoon light
oak leaves falling from the weight
of their gold
a teen with Down Syndrome
strokes his mother's face

    Claire Everett
    (UK)

Runners-up

hard to believe
that I'm closer to the end
than the beginning
the things that can't be undone
the ones that never will be

     John Soules
     (Canada)

it's not right
to have to bury
your children
their days too short
the nights too long

     John Soules
     (Canada)

Runners-up

day after day
scouring the wreckage
for survivors—
my mother no longer
remembers my name

David Terelinck
(Australia)

then the wind
plucks a rusted lid
from the garbage can...
once again you tell me
how it meant nothing

David Terelinck
(Australia)

Runners-up

I lie awake
and listen to the small noises
of my neighbours
the calls of city birds
late into the night

    Alison Williams
    (UK

in the evening
of a long, hot
summer day
a stranger's shadow
merges with mine

    Alison Williams
    (UK)

Runners-up

as each day passes
the sea changes the land
but with each passed day
the changed land changes the sea...
a sculptor moulded by their clay

David J.Kelly
(Ireland)

childhood friends
fewer and fewer moments
in common
across our divide
your news still touches me

David J. Kelly
(Ireland)

Runners-up

on a park bench
a blind man and his white cane
seeing beyond sight
his fingers on
this city's pulse

David J. Kelly
(Ireland)

our last season
is catching up with us
the appearance
of snow at my temples
skeletons in your closet

an'ya
(USA)

Runners-up

we build our foundations
wattle and daub
memories packed tight
the tempestuous cloud
a mere shadow away

Joanna Ashwell
(UK)

how many ghosts
are yet to haunt me
in the years to come?
the dawn river swollen
by a night full of rain

John Barlow
(UK)

Runners-up

unkempt garden
my father bends
to capture the butterfly
his presence
as fragile as its wings

Rebecca Brown
(UK)

running his fingernails
down the old school blackboard
still wondering
why he has
so few friends

Peter Butler
(UK)

Runners-up

Roma boys
rummage through the dump site
for scrap metal
riverside fireworks
light the summer sky

> Chen-ou Liu
> (Canada)

tongue running
over tooth-pulled gums
i cheer myself up
with a novocaine grin
that scares the cat

> David Cox
> (UK)

Runners-up

an evening
sifting through
family photos...
hearing the waves
wash in,wash out

Dawn Bruce
(Australia)

your overgrown shed
long undisturbed hinges
rusting silently
inside a thousand spiders
still listen for your footsteps

David Davies
(UK)

Runners-up

on the edge
of Skeleton Wood
the nightjar churrs—
in rising mist
a slow train passes

    Tim Gardiner
    (UK)

midnight tears
closing one eye
I raise a hand
pointing a finger
I block out a star

    Kevin Goldstein-Jackson
    (UK)

Runners-up

a purple puffer
already helping me
breathe in...
what will help
breathe out the anger?

Carole Harrison
(Australia)

I keep busy
waiting for your return
from her—
bees collect the last
late autumn nectar

Marilyn Humbert
(Australia)

Runners-up

you hear them coming
like wasps trapped in a tin can
the Lambretta boys
zooming past they leave behind
blue plumes of two stroke oil

    Lee Jackson
    (UK)

I remove
the sheets of wallpaper
one by one
finding beneath the veneer
unexpected imperfections

    Elaine Riddell
    (New Zealand)

Runners-up

so late
his birthday bouquet
fragrant
with good wishes
and a hint of guilt

Susan King
(UK)

Polaris once guided
the prisoner-of-war home:
great granddad
in long term care asks
if he has always lived here

Beth McFarland
(Germany)

Runners-up

the wonder
of flying weightless
in the big top
a moth flutters high
up to the spotlight

       Vanessa Proctor
       (Australia)

migrating geese
writing cursive letters
across the sky
I finally read between
the white of your lies

       Debbie Strange
       (Canada)

Runners-up

autumn mist
a contour of the heron
in the stream
a passer-by on the bridge
pacing very much like you

      Đurđa Vukelić Rožić
      (Croatia)

snow dusts the barn
crumpled into itself
—inscribed to you
   the poems you returned
   in a stack of unread books

      Linda Jeannette Ward
      (USA)

Runners-up

she waved to me
the lady on the jetty
looking out to sea
the wind blew her hair around
as my ship sailed away

       Mark Warren
       (UK)

alone
I return
nothing has changed
but a single flower
withered in a vase

       Robert Witmer
       (Japan)